# OLD CAT

Written and Illustrated by
## Barbara Libby

GRAMERCY BOOKS
New York • Avenel, New Jersey

*To Mort*

Published by Gramercy Books
distributed by Outlet Book Company, Inc.,
a Random House Company,
40 Engelhard Avenue
Avenel, New Jersey  07001

Random House
New York · Toronto · London · Sydney · Auckland

Printed and bound in the United States

**Library of Congress Cataloging-in-Publication Data**
Libby, Barbara.
Old cat / written and illustrated by Barbara Libby.
p.   cm.
ISBN 0-517-09324-3
1. Cats--Anecdotes.  2. Libby, Barbara.  I. Title.
SF445.5.L53   1993
636.8--dc20                    93-17311
CIP

8  7  6  5  4  3  2  1

He is an old cat.
He sleeps long hours beneath the bedroom rocker
  cushioned by woolly brown carpet.
Our old cat likes the small cave the chair makes, underneath,
  so we never move it.
He sleeps, no longer alert to car brakes
  squeaking in driveways, keys clicking in locks,
  or can openers signaling dinnertime.

Rackety children crashing down stairs.
Bikes, bats,
autos, houses, dogs—
it's a wonder I survived
my kittenhood on that street.

I found safety under shrubbery
and watched our door for
goings and comings.
You never knew what happened
when I disappeared for weeks,
but it was good to see you again
I can tell you that.

He is an old prowler.
He leaps only for worthwhile reasons:
   afternoon sunlight,
   the blue chenille robe
   I leave on my bed.
It is my favorite bathrobe, thick as a blanket.
If he is not on it
   I'll borrow it briefly,
   replace it gently,
   for my old cat to curl up in again.

That apartment winter I paced room to room,
leaped floor to sill,
watching from windows.
In spring you let me out at last!
The wooded patch beside the drive
was mine, but it was perilous.  I took
a pellet in the thigh from some child
imagining lions,
and that tough orange tom got me
once or twice.
I claimed some of his fur as well!

Locked in that garage for days,
I heard you calling.
Cold cement.
Cold, dirty water.
Not much else.
When the door finally opened
I headed home,
starving,
for food
and your shoulder.

Who purred louder, you or I?

He is an old mouser
   who now surveys his grounds indoors
   from sunny windows.
It is a territory measured in rooms, not acres,
   in warm carpets and wood fires,
   not honeysuckle and tall grass.
As cardinals peck sunflower seed
   and goldfinches dive for thistle
   outside the living-room window,
   he stretches—
   and settles more comfortably
   on the couch.

A small house
in woods that went on forever,
with covered porches to wait out the rain.
Small, silent panther stalking through milkweed,
the black ears, back, and tail of me
would disappear against the night,
while legs and underbelly glowed blue-white.
I felt invisible!

One night a field rat
gnawed,
slithered
through cracks,
to the space beneath your bed.
I sniffed it out—
hissed,
spit!
Clawed it out!

You and I shared the bed after that.
But sometimes I'd place a mouse,
or a mole,
carefully on the step,
just to remind you
how well I did my job.

He is an old veteran,
    less handsome than he used to be:
    a single green eye,
    stiff bony back, and fur
    a used muff that's seen better days.
I hardly notice.
As with any dear friend,
    it's the soul inside I see,
    not the worn surface.

We moved
deeper into the woods
and higher.
Beneath tall oaks, you built a house
with high decks
for surveying the woods around.
And I was a grand leaper,
landing foursquare on the deck railing
twenty feet above ground!

Ambling its length,
I'd come within range
of the bird feeder
that sits at one corner.
You'd rush out the door if you saw me!
I'd just saunter off, tail high.
There were woods to explore—
rabbits and moles
and white-footed mice!
And the birds
would be there tomorrow.
So would I.

He is an old explorer.
He finds paths around hillsides of quilt
   and discovers small valleys to nest in, between.
I always make room for him.
Between my knee and pillow,
   he circles and circles.
My old cat settles slowly in the middle of the night,
   but rewards my patience
   with smooth purring in my ear.

My paws
knew every inch of woods,
from creek to oak, and
warren to nest.
Where blue jays live,
black rat snakes, and squirrels.
Where deer cross.
Where rabbits hide.
It's all been fine,
the quiet times too—
warm milk,
Sundays on the couch.

Remember our stories
when fur and bones
and tail of me are gone.
Share them with
some young new mouser, who'll
need to learn
where blue jays live,
where rabbits hide. . .
who'll share your couch
and bowls of milk,
who'll be your friend. . .
though maybe
not as good a friend
as I.